OSAKA
THE CITY AT A G

MW01005917

Osaka Station
Dating from 1874 and pa
that encompasses Umeda Station, this is the
principal railway terminal in the north, with
links to Kobe and Kyoto. Overhauled in 2011,
it neighbours the Grand Front development.
3-1-1 Umeda

Hilton Plaza
The chic mall is split between two buildings.
Check out the Louis Vuitton store (West 1F,
T 03 3478 2100), whose facade was devised
by architect Kumiko Inui, and call in to B Bar
(East 2F, T 06 6341 2375) for a pick-me-up.
East, 1-8-16 Umeda; West, 2-2-2 Umeda

Breezé Tower
Dine at Zipangu (T 06 4797 3311) atop this
177m-tall skyscraper designed by Christoph
Ingenhoven for views as inspiring as the food.
2-4-9 Umeda, T 06 6343 1633

Herbis Plaza
Hirsch Bedner Associates' mixed-use high-
rise redefined the station area in 1997. The 40
storeys above ground include The Ritz-Carlton
(see p022). Its sibling is the 2004 Herbis Ent.
2-5-25 Umeda, T 06 6343 7500

Hanshin Expressway
Ugly but necessary in this densely populated
city, the 240km of expressways constructed
high above ground level help ensure Osaka's
roads are less traffic-clogged and the streets
below more pedestrian-friendly.

Gate Tower Building
The expressway couldn't be built around this
16-floor tower, known locally as the Beehive
and completed in 1992, so it curves straight
through levels five to seven instead. Genius.
5-4-21 Fukushima

INTRODUCTION
THE CHANGING FACE OF THE URBAN SCENE

Osaka was, long ago and rather briefly, the capital of Japan. Most locals are more likely to tell you that it's the birthplace of instant ramen. This is an unsentimental place, driven by commerce, with few landmarks to lure in tourists. Consequently, not many visitors take the 15-minute *shinkansen* ride from Kyoto, whose measured elegance offers a dramatic counterpoint to its boisterous neighbour.

They are missing out. This is one of the most vibrant cities in the country. Its inhabitants are noisy, nosy, warm and entertaining. In Tokyo and Kyoto, people mind their own business. In Osaka, they'll grill you about yours. It's not a glamorous destination, and there is no coherent aesthetic. But that has given architects the freedom to play. Pritzker Prize-winners Kenzo Tange and Tadao Ando grew up here, and Ando in particular has had a say in how it looks today.

The metropolis has been expanding since WWII. Unlike Tokyo, which frequently looks to the US for inspiration, it is becoming a world player in a distinctly Japanese way, and is a hotbed of talent. Its creative scene is promoted in cafés and bookshops, street fashion remains organic and design enterprises that were born here have tended to stay. A stroll through the unnamed lanes of downtown Horie will tell you all you need to know about the future: the old men's noodle shops continue to do a roaring trade, but many of the eateries, studios and galleries are filled with a new generation of Osakans quietly plotting out their hometown's next step.

ESSENTIAL INFO
FACTS, FIGURES AND USEFUL ADDRESSES

TOURIST OFFICE
Visitors' Information Center
JR Osaka Station
3-1-1 Umeda
www.osaka-info.jp

TRANSPORT
Airport transfer to city centre
The Kansai-Airport Express Haruka reaches
Tennoji Station in about 30 minutes
www.hyperdia.com
Car hire
Hertz
T 06 6933 1461
Taxi
MK Taxi
T 06 6452 4441
Tourist card
A two-day Osaka Amazing Pass grants
unlimited travel and access to museums
www.osaka-info.jp

EMERGENCY SERVICES
Ambulance/Fire
T 119
Police
T 110
24-hour pharmacy
Familymart+ Kusuri Higuchi Kyobashi
5-1-16 Higashinodamachi
T 06 6882 4193

CONSULATES
British Consulate-General
19F, Epson Osaka Building
3-5-1 Bakuro-machi
T 06 6120 5600
www.gov.uk/government/world/japan
US Consulate-General
2-11-5 Nishitenma
T 06 6315 5900
jp.usembassy.gov/embassy-consulates/osaka

POSTAL SERVICES
Post office
Osaka Ekimae Daiichi Building
1-3-1 Umeda
T 05 7000 3280
Shipping
UPS
3-3-16 Ishida
T 06 4395 6707

BOOKS
**Beyond the Bubble: The New Japanese
Architecture** by Botond Bognar (Phaidon)
**Tadao Ando: The Colours of Light
Volume 1** by Richard Pare (Phaidon)

WEBSITES
Architecture
www.au-magazine.com
Art
www.digmeout.net
Newspaper
www.japantimes.co.jp

EVENTS
Art Osaka
www.artosaka.jp
Tenjin Festival
www.japan.travel/spot/30

COST OF LIVING
**Taxi from Kansai International
Airport to city centre**
¥15,000
Cappuccino
¥450
Packet of cigarettes
¥450
Daily newspaper
¥250
Bottle of champagne
¥15,000

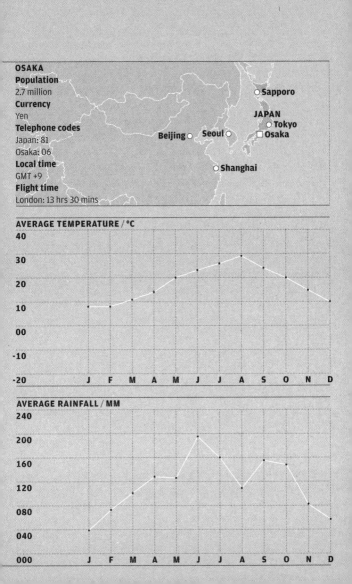

OSAKA
Population
2.7 million
Currency
Yen
Telephone codes
Japan: 81
Osaka: 06
Local time
GMT +9
Flight time
London: 13 hrs 30 mins

○ Sapporo

JAPAN
○ Tokyo
Beijing ○   Seoul ○   □ Osaka

○ Shanghai

AVERAGE TEMPERATURE / °C

40
30
20
10
00
-10
-20

J F M A M J J A S O N D

AVERAGE RAINFALL / MM

240
200
160
120
080
040
000

J F M A M J J A S O N D

NEIGHBOURHOODS
THE AREAS YOU NEED TO KNOW AND WHY

To help you navigate the city, we've chosen the most interesting districts (see below and the map inside the back cover) and colour-coded our featured venues, according to their location; those venues that are outside these areas are not coloured.

MINAMI
This rapidly evolving district is a creative flashpoint. The broad Mido-suji shopping strip is lined with major brands housed in architecturally interesting buildings. Head for Horie and Minamisemba, where there are cafés packed with hipsters and young professionals on every corner. The Glico Man (see p014) is a lesson in marketing savvy and Namba Parks (see p065) is an example of how to make a mall work.

KITA
Centred around the northern section of Mido-suji, this neighbourhood is defined by skyscrapers, hotels, including The Ritz-Carlton (see p022), restaurants, such as Fukutatei (see p052), underground malls, theatres and Osaka Station. The Umeda Sky Building (see p011) is a long-standing icon, Hankyu Men's (7-10 Kakuda-cho, T 06 6361 1381) is a slick department store and the Grand Front complex is another draw.

NAKANOSHIMA
Its international feel makes Nakanoshima almost seem part of an entirely different city. Osaka's business centre is peppered with Western-style architecture and large gardens. The National Museum of Art (see p029) is a highlight and the stately Central Public Hall (1-1-27 Nakanoshima) sits on the banks of the Tosabori River. It's a great area for a watery stroll; stop for coffee at Moto (see p042) or Brooklyn Roasting Company (2-1-16 Kitahama, T 06 6125 5740).

OSAKA CASTLE
The castle (see p015) marks the site of the city's founding and is encircled by green space, dotted with cherry trees that burst into life each spring. The park stretches up to the Hirano River in the north – on its opposite bank rise the contemporary towers of Osaka Business Park. Be sure to visit the Museum of History (4-1-32 Otemae, T 06 6946 5728), designed by Cesar Pelli, a fascinating study of the past 1,350 years.

THE BAY
Once an industrial port, The Bay is being reinvented as an entertainment district. But it still has a long way to go, and many local shops and restaurants here are past their prime. However, there's some striking architecture, in particular Osaka Pool (Koen Nai, 3-1-20 Tanaka, T 06 6571 2010), which has a highly impressive flexible fabric roof, Cosmo Tower (see p010) and the madcap Maishima Incineration Plant (see p074).

TENNOJI
Tourists come to downtown Tennoji to see two of its landmarks – Shitennoji Temple (1-11-18 Shitenno-ji), first built in the late 6th century, and the eyesore Tsutenkaku Tower (see p009) – then quickly head back to more graceful environs. But the area is being regenerated and now boasts one of Japan's tallest structures, Abeno Harukas (see p012). Set within Tennoji Park, you'll find the Osaka City Museum of Fine Arts (1-82 Chausuyama-cho, T 06 6771 4874).

LANDMARKS

THE SHAPE OF THE CITY SKYLINE

The engine room of Japanese industry during WWII, Osaka was pounded by fire-bombing raids that left its predominantly timber structures incinerated and a good many brick edifices destroyed. But the metropolis was quickly resuscitated after the war, and soon regained its position as a commercial centre and port. Among the buildings to be reconstructed was Daimaru (1-7-1 Shinsaibashi-suji, T 06 6271 1231), the principal department store. Other landmarks, such as the enormous electronic billboard depicting Glico Man (see p014), symbol of the confectionery firm, and Gaetano Pesce's Organic Building (see p076), play key roles in this maze-like town, often providing visitors with their only reference point when they are attempting to locate a well-hidden café or temple.

A structure that will never win a beauty prize is the 103m-tall Tsutenkaku Tower (1-18-6 Ebisu-Higashi, T 06 6641 9555), which is used as advertising space by Hitachi. Much easier on the eye is Hiroshi Hara's Umeda Sky Building (see p011). Started in 1988, in the era of Japan's bubble economy when the country was awash with cash, this was envisaged as a city in the sky, where high-rises would support a plateau of gardens, retail outlets and walkways. But the bubble burst and only two towers connected by a viewing platform were completed. It's an impressive sight nonetheless, and stands proud as Osaka's first piece of destination architecture. *For full addresses, see Resources.*

Cosmo Tower

The 55th-floor observation deck at the tip of this tower remains uncrowded owing to its out-of-the-way location at Osaka Port on the reclaimed island of Sakishima. The thrill of the non-stop 80-second ride up to the top in the high-velocity glazed elevator is worth the trip on its own; the panorama of Awaji Island, Mount Rokko and back over the bay to the city centre provides the icing on the cake. Nicknamed the Cosmo Tower, known as Osaka World Trade Center until 2010, and now officially recognised as the Osaka Prefectural Government Sakishima Building, it was designed by Nikken Sekkei and completed in 1995. A glass curtain wall with white mullions emphasises the height of the 256m-tall skyscraper. At its base it widens into a triangular shape that echoes the inverted pyramid at its crown.

1-14-16 Nankokita, Suminoe-ku

Umeda Sky Building

This 40-storey building, comprising twin high-rises connected at the top two levels, redefined Osaka and gave it a focal point. Conceived by Hiroshi Hara and completed in 1993, it draws about one million people every year, who marvel at its implausible design and soak in the 360-degree views from 173m up on the roof. A postmodern take on the Hanging Gardens of Babylon, it is bordered to the north and south by verdant tree-lined paths. Hara believes that the towers may yet serve as a jumping-off point for a brand-new layer above the city: an elevated public network that would link its skyscrapers in the air. For an indoor vista, head to Cafe Sky 40 on the top floor, secure a window seat, order an aperitif and watch the sun set over the Yodo River.
1-1-88 Oyodonaka, T 06 6440 3855,
www.skybldg.co.jp

Abeno Harukas

Cesar Pelli devised several of the city's most distinctive structures, including the Osaka Museum of History (T 06 6946 5728) and The National Museum of Art (see p029). His final contribution to the urban fabric may not be his best work but it is the biggest. At 300m, the 2014 Abeno Harukas skyscraper is one of Japan's tallest buildings, topping The Landmark Tower in Yokohama by 4m. The tiered high-rise is enveloped in glass and steel. Within, it's a mixed-use complex that encompasses a department store, a two-level observation deck, a modern art museum and a 360-room Marriott hotel (T 06 6628 6111). The structure is owned by railway company Kintetsu. The firm is hoping that Abeno Harukas does the same for the dowdy Tennoji district as the Mori Tower in Tokyo did for reborn Roppongi.
1-1-43 Abeno-suji,
www.abenoharukas-300.jp

Glico Man Sign

Dotonbori fulfils all the fantasies of those who come to Japan in search of the kind of scenes depicted in *Blade Runner*. At night, the corridor flickers into life as dozens of neon billboards, some as big as multistorey buildings, are activated. But for Osakans, only one matters: the 20m-tall Glico Man, who appears arms aloft over a street-side canal. Erected in 1935, he is also known as the '300m runner', after the distance that the calories in one piece of Glico candy are said to propel you. At its base is Ebisubashi Bridge, a popular hangout for teens. It is also the spot where fans of local baseball outfit the Hanshin Tigers line up to strike Glico Man's victory pose and jump into the murky waters below when their team wins the league. The design has gone through various iterations and is now lit by LEDs.
1-10-2 Dotonbori-dori

Osaka Castle

The depressing truth about Osaka Castle is that it's fake. What's more, the current building, erected in 1931 and renovated in 1997, isn't even a faithful replica of the original 1583 structure – and it's made of concrete. But maybe that's appropriate, as the story of the edifice is one of continual destruction and reconstruction. It was expanded between 1620 and 1629; struck by lightning in 1665; razed again in 1868; remade using reinforced concrete in the 1930s; bombed in WWII; and restored in the 1990s. Located within a 60,000 sq m site encompassing the former Osaka City Museum, its seven storeys house displays of samurai armour and weaponry, and a tea room. The landmark is big and brash, and perfectly embodies the local spirit. *1-1 Osakajo, T 06 6941 3044, www.osakacastle.net*

HOTELS

WHERE TO STAY AND WHICH ROOMS TO BOOK

Osaka has been a trade hub for more than 500 years, yet its hotel scene failed to make the transition from ryokans to Western-style accommodation, leaving imports, such as The New Otani (1-4-1 Shiromi, T 06 6941 1111), the Imperial (1-8-50 Tenmabashi, T 06 6881 1111) and The Westin (1-1-20 Oyodonaka, T 06 6440 1111) to fill the void. The global chains can be hit and miss; exceptions are The Ritz-Carlton (see p022), the St Regis (3-6-12 Honmachi, T 06 6258 3333) and the Conrad (3-2-4 Nakanoshima, T 06 6222 0111), although even these can be a little lacking in character. Offering more of a local experience are the accomplished boutique options Moxy (opposite) and The Flag (see p020), while The Grandee (1-6-28 Higashi-Shinsaibashi, T 06 6251 7170) comprises some of the most eccentric rooms in town: 812 boasts a rock garden and tree trunk, and 713 has an aquarium and illuminated 'firefly' bathtub. Osaka was the birthplace of the capsule hotel but it's always had a dearth of attractive budget properties. Addressing that gap is the airline-themed First Cabin (4-2-1 Namba, T 06 6631 8090).

The ambience at a ryokan can be daunting for visitors who don't speak Japanese or are unfamiliar with customs concerning dining or bathing – Yamatoya Honten (2-17-4 Shimanouchi, T 06 6211 3587) is a foreigner-friendly choice. Note that many Osakans smoke, so specify when booking if you'd like to avoid the smell of tobacco. *For full addresses and room rates, see Resources.*

Moxy

This hip hangout, opened in 2017, hollers at passers-by with its hot-pink signage above the entrance. Designed for sociable young travellers, the 155-room property has the convivial atmosphere of a swish hostel but none of the drawbacks. Kitted out by Tokyo studio Wise Labo, the double-height lobby features mismatched furniture, graffiti by local artist Zenone and a piece by sculptor Hideyuki Matsuda. The compact pads have modular layouts with foldable furnishings. The peg system by Yabu Pushelberg, used in Moxy ventures globally, serves in place of a wardrobe. If you want more space, opt for one of the 18 Signature Queens (above). The house cocktail, available at the 24-hour café/bar, is a heady blend of Chivas Regal, lime, coriander, mint and ginger ale.
2-2-9 Kawaramachi, T 06 6204 5200, www.marriott.com

Residential Hotel Hare Kuromon

Opened in 2018, this condo-style bolthole fuses the new and the nostalgic. From the *noren* draped across its entrance to the 15 *tatami*-floored rooms with *shoji* doors and windows, RHHK embodies the aesthetic of the traditional home without skimping on function and convenience. The apartment-style accommodations are equipped with a kitchenette and a washing machine, as well as a luxurious handmade ceramic bathtub from celebrated pottery region Shigaraki. Each can sleep up to four on a combination of Western beds and Japanese futons; the biggest, Type D, has an expansive balcony. There is coffee in the foyer, outfitted with 'Dino Lounge' chairs by Idée, but no dining option. Instead, pop in to nearby Cafe & Bar HRR (T 06 6648 8676), which closes late. *2-14-32 Nipponbashi, T 06 4394 8708, www.hotelhare.jp/kuromon*

Hotel She

Maverick hotelier Shoko Ryuzaki launched her first property while still a student and now has outposts across Japan. The Kyoto native opened this intimate 'social hotel' in the formerly working-class harbour district of Bentencho in 2017. Its palette reflects its roots and there are hues of midnight blue throughout the one-time apartment block, from the tiles on the facade to the exposed brickwork on the ground floor. Osaka studio Atode fitted out the inviting interiors. The lobby (above) features 'H760' stools by Neri & Hu, 'IL-02' chairs by Takayama firm Kitani and original oak flooring, and the 46 rooms have comfy Simmons mattresses, works by local artists, including photographer Yuki Nobuhara, and record players; head to the 'library' to choose from a selection of LPs. *1-2-5 Ichioka, Minato-ku, T 06 6577 5500, www.hotelsheosaka.com*

The Flag
A welcome relief from the non-stop bustle
of the nearby Shinsaibashi shopping strip,
this slick nine-storey hotel opened in 2018
in a former care home renovated by locals
Process5 Design. Natural materials appear
throughout. Enter via the automatic sliding
door fashioned from dried horse-chestnut
wood from the north of the country, and
take the lift to the reception area, which is
anchored by a massive decorative boulder
inset with a small native tree. The adjoining
lobby (opposite) is a calming environment;
settle into an Eames 'Lounge Chair' beside
the mesmerising bioethanol fire. The 162
understated, well-organised rooms, such
as the Deluxe Double (above), are finished
in melamine laminate to counter scratches.
At breakfast, Be.zen offers seasonal dishes
and international fare including *pot-au-feu*
on tableware sourced from across Japan.
1-18-30 Higashi-Shinsaibashi,
T 06 6121 8111, www.hoteltheflag.jp

The Ritz-Carlton

To inject a novel flavour into the local hotel scene, this handsome hideaway in a section of the 40-storey Herbis boasts a distinctly Western look. Common areas are modelled on a Georgian townhouse, doormen wear hats and tails, and the swish lobby features paintings by Peter MacNab and Henry John Yeend King, mahogany mouldings, Italian marble and Persian carpets. In the British-style pads, bespoke furniture by Baker and a mellow palette of cream and blue keep things plush, and there are also two sleek Japanese Suites (above) that offer classic ryokan hallmarks; all rooms have a super panorama of downtown. Of the warren of eateries here, we recommend Hanagatami, which serves five different cuisines, from teppanyaki to Michelin-starred tempura.
2-5-25 Umeda, T 06 6343 7000,
www.ritzcarlton.com/osaka

The Blend Inn

Architect Yo Shimada, head of Kobe firm Tato, devised this guest house/hotel from the ground up, leaving the concrete block with a deliberately unfinished feel — walls are unpainted and wiring is exposed. It is a riff on the creative vibe of the local area, and a side street was incorporated into the design to blur the boundary between public and private. The communal lounge (above) has some unique furniture such as the zinc chromate-coated 'Lotus Leaves Table', and hosts rotating exhibitions, for instance, the work of photographer Chikashi Kasai. The small kitchen is available to use outside of breakfast hours. Its seven rooms take their titles from songs by The Beach Boys, Fatboy Slim and other acts, and the raw shells are softened by bespoke beds and art pieces.
1-24-16 Baika, Konohana-ku,
T 070 1745 1250, www.theblend.jp

24 HOURS

SEE THE BEST OF THE CITY IN JUST ONE DAY

Osaka lacks a tourist trail, which allows you free rein to get under its skin. To keep things simple, start south and move north. Wake yourself up at Granknot (opposite) or Lilo Coffee Roasters (1-10-28 Nishishinsaibashi), close to the bizarre street fashion outlets on Triangle Park. Browse the furniture and homewares stores, including Biotop (see p083), along Tachibana-dori (Orange Street), and the loud, poptastic Shinsabashisuji Shotengai, a covered arcade of fast commerce, which leads you to the Glico Man (see p014). Around here there's street food galore, cobbled Hozenji Yokocho is a dining enclave, Wasabi (see p047) specialises in local favourite *kushikatsu* and Kigawa (1-7-7 Dotonbori, T 06 6211 3030) serves *kappo*-style cuisine (*omakase* that's less formal and expensive than *kaiseki*).

Make your way to Nakazakicho, a creative pocket of vintage and handicraft stores near Umeda Station; Salon de Amanto (1-7-26 Nakazakinishi, T 06 6371 5840), an arts café in an 1880s building, is ground zero. By night, the latern-lit alleys of Tenma Ichiba teem with mom-and-pop eateries and specialist bars, such as Beer Belly (1-1-31 Tosaburi, T 06 6441 0717), for Osakan craft brews. Go upmarket with cocktails at Kaara (see p031), gin at Bar Juniper (1-4-4 Dojima, T 06 6348 0414) or aged liqueur at Elixir K (1-2-9 Dojima, T 080 9168 9502), and finish up at Noon+Cafe (3-3-8 Nakazakinishi, T 06 6373 4919), which regularly hosts DJ sessions and live electronica acts. *For full addresses, see Resources.*

10.00 Granknot Coffee Roasters

The baristas behind Granknot, opened in 2013, honed their trade in an Umeda café and, after learning about the trailblazing Stumptown model in Portland, decided to do something similar. Design studio Antry devised the branding and decked out the interior with reclaimed furniture – there are tables made from salvaged wooden planks and chairs sourced from a church in the US. Owners Katsuya Shibano and Hideaki Takahashi then added their own creative flourishes, including the snaking copper pipes repurposed as wall-mounted light fixtures. The pair partnered up with a local roaster to produce a custom coffee blend, which is brewed with Hario V60 or Saint Anthony Industries C70 drippers, or a La Marzocco machine. To eat, there are muffins and doughnuts. Closed Thursdays.
1-23-4 Kita-Horie, T 06 6531 6020

11.30 Shiba Ryotaro Memorial Museum
Local scribe Shiba Ryotaro authored about 500 historical novels and cultural essays and is a key figure in Japanese literature. This architectural memorial was unveiled in Higashiosaka in 2001, next to the house he occupied until he passed away in 1996, and was devised by Tadao Ando to invite visitors into the writer's mind. Approach the curved glass-fronted volume, much of which was built underground, through the landscaped garden, in which Ryotaro used to meditate. Inside, natural light diminishes towards the centrepiece (opposite), which is illuminated via a solitary white-tinted window. The walls are lined with 11m-high bookshelves that display Ryotaro's 20,000-strong collection. You can also peer into his study from outside. Closed Mondays.
3-11-18 Shimokosaka, Higashiosaka,
T 06 6726 3860, www.shibazaidan.or.jp

14.00 Artcourt Gallery

This renowned 2003 gallery set within the gardens of the OAP (Osaka Amenity Park) Tower celebrates luminaries of postwar art such as conceptualist Hitoshi Nomura, whose works often overlap with science, and Saburo Murakami and Norio Imai of the radical Gutai group. Its double-height interior also provides a platform for the new generation including Satoshi Kawata, who questioned the permanence of the mural by painting on hanging cloth in the exhibition 'Open Room'. Shows like 'Twiggy Project' (above), a set of vegetal steel-and-glass forms by Osakan Keiju Kawashima, often spill out into the central courtyard. Closed Sundays and Mondays. New works are installed every 18 months or so on the riverside OAP Sculpture Path.
1-8-5 Tenmabashi, T 06 6354 5444, www.artcourtgallery.com

16.00 The National Museum of Art

Inaugurated in 1977 in the Expo park on the city outskirts, The National was moved to this central location in 2004. A three-floor structure buried on an island, crowned by a symphony of steel tubes, Osakans call it the 'submarine', whereas Cesar Pelli, the late architect responsible for its audacious design, dubbed it 'a bathtub, in a bathtub, in a bathtub'. Either way, it certainly made a splash. The lower levels are enshrined in walls that are extra thick in case the river should meander in another direction. The museum's collection numbers thousands of works, including pieces by photographer Hiroshi Sugimoto and Mono-ha artist Nobuo Sekine, while a past temporary exhibition reexamined the Japanese new wave that emerged in the 1980s. Closed Mondays. *4-2-55 Nakanoshima, T 06 6447 4680, www.nmao.go.jp*

19.00 HEP Five

A giant red Ferris wheel atop a 10-storey edifice may seem a crazy idea, but it is an arresting combination and one of the city's iconic sights. Completed in 1998, HEP Five was designed and built by local engineering firm Takenaka Corporation, which dates to 1610 and has worked with architects of the calibre of Toyo Ito, Tadao Ando, Herzog & de Meuron and Cesar Pelli. The 15-minute ride, which reaches a height of 106m, starts on the seventh floor and glides past several levels of high-energy retail madness before its air-conditioned gondolas take to the sky. Inside the shopping mall, more than 100 boutiques and a VR arcade cater to Osakan teens who have a penchant for flamboyant outfits and like to immortalise themselves in the *purikura* booths on the eighth storey. *5-15 Kakuda-cho, T 06 6313 0501, www.hepfive.jp*

22.00 Kaara

First, head to two-Michelin-starred Kahala (T 06 6345 6778), run by Yoshifumi Mori, to dine on *karasumi* soba and beef millefeuille at its 8.40pm seating. Then visit this cosy bar, also run by Mori, to sample the superb concoctions created by Koukichi Takahashi with the kind of artistry and precision for which the country's mixologists are known. Some of the cocktails are served in antique glasses and others have more unorthodox presentations: the speciality gin and tonic comes in an inverted lime skin – the sour tang and essential oils of the peel giving it an added zing. The interiors feature a low *washi* ceiling, exposed brick and dark wood, and a counter fashioned from a single piece of Japanese elm. Kaara can hold just eight people and there are no reservations, but it does stay open until 2am. Closed Sundays.
6F, 1-1-18 Sonezaki-Shinchi, T 06 6341 2818

URBAN LIFE

CAFÉS, RESTAURANTS, BARS AND NIGHTCLUBS

Osakans coined a word to illustrate their attitude to food: *kuidaore*, which translates roughly as 'eat until you drop'. Proud epicureans, they use it to distinguish themselves from their Kyoto neighbours (more obsessed with clothing and homewares) and Tokyo rivals.

The stereotype is of a city filled with cheap, frenetic places firing out local dishes such as *takoyaki* (octopus dumplings), *okonomiyaki* (egg, flour and cabbage pancakes topped with meat and vegetables), *kushikatsu* (fried cutlets on a bamboo skewer) and udon noodles, but dining here is more bountiful than this. High up on the splurge list is Michelin-starred Sushi Yoshi (2-3-23 Minamimorimachi, T 06 6361 0062), chef Hiroki Nakanoue's creative *omakase* experience, while the outlook for non-carnivores has dramatically improved: Paprika Shokudo (1-9-9 Shinmachi, T 06 6599 9788) serves clever organic vegan dishes in a charming setting. Top-tier establishments that open for lunch often offer bargain prices, and so office workers descend between noon and 1pm in the week; arrive after the crush.

Nightlife is flash and brash, and Shinsaibashi is the area in which to drink, dance and sing karaoke – prepare at ritzy cocktail bar The Suite (2-18-18 Nishishinsaibashi, T 06 6282 7742), designed like a 1920s New York lounge. Comodo (4F, 1-17-15 Higashi-Shinsaibashi, T 06 6258 8088) hosts intimate jazz performances; explore the gig scene at Socore Factory (2-13-26 Minami-Horie, T 06 6567 9852). *For full addresses, see Resources.*

Ad Hoc

Chef Tatsuhiro Takayama trained at Japan's most famous cooking school, Tsuji Culinary Institute, before working in Osaka's French restaurants and then launching his own, the casual bistro Tout-Le-Monde, in 2002. After evolving into a more refined offering, it was shuttered in 2014, only to reopen in nearby Nakanoshima under a new name. Meant to evoke a Normandy barn, it was designed by Hiroyuki Ogura of local firm Drawers, and interiors feature exposed beams made of century-old wood, NYC studio Workstead's 'Industrial Chandelier' and custom-made Hans Wegner-style chairs. For the tasting menus, only three or four components are used to create each beautifully presented course, such as seaweed-wrapped Wagyu served with leeks and *shijimi* clam sauce. *1-1-48 Fukushima, T 06 6225 8814, www.adhoc2014.jp*

Shuhari

Yosuke Hashimoto kickstarted his Osaka chain of soba restaurants with this 40-seat branch in 2008. Fitted out by locals Design Ground 55, it features small tables made of elm from Hokkaido prefecture, as well as a central counter of reclaimed conifer wood. The traditional Japanese mud walls, built by city firm Generation X, play nicely with the modern 'Solaris' light fixtures by Nara-based New Light Pottery. You can observe the soba masters kneading and cutting the strands, made from buckwheat flour and milled each morning, through the window. The menu comprises *zarusoba* (served cold on a bamboo basket), tempura dishes and umami-suffused *dashi maki tamago* (rolled omelette). There's also fresh wasabi, which you can grate yourself, and a range of sake.
1-3-20 Tokiwamachi, T 06 6944 8808, shuhari.main.jp

Sumibi Kappo Ishii

Conspicuous for its Mondrian-like exterior (a white facade divided by dark beams), this charcoal-grill eaterie is located on a quiet side street not far from its Michelin-starred sister venue Torisho Ishii (T 06 4797 1129). Inside, a bamboo-lined pathway christened after Kyoto strip Kiyamachi-dori leads into the calming interior, all wooden panels and matcha-green walls. References to the old capital continue in the carpentry, and there is a painting by artist Ryohei Miwa hanging behind the long *hinoki* counter. At the core of Ryuji Nonohara's umami-rich cooking are *katsuobushi* (dried bonito flakes). The *omakase* menu might include saltwater eel seasoned with sansho powder, sea bream rice, scorched shellfish or tiger prawn soup prepared using homemade dashi.
7-17-11 Fukushima, Fukushima-ku,
T 06 7708 4692

Honkogetsu

This two-Michelin-starred bellwether is the template for contemporary *kaiseki*, from the wonderfully restrained interiors and procession of beautifully ornate serving plates and paraphernalia, some of which is centuries old, to the variety and thrill of ingredients and tastes. Chef Hideo Anami took over the then-named Kogetsu in 1974 when he was only 25, and has been at the helm ever since. His menus, typically 11 or 12 courses, might encompass horsehair crab from Funka Bay in Hokkaido, *tachiika* squid from the Seto Inland Sea prepared three ways, and specialities like dried sea-cucumber ovaries. A fire razed the building in 2002. For its reopening four years later, Anami installed a centrepiece 600-year-old *hinoki* wood counter, as well as a basement to store the vast collection of tableware.
1-7-11 Dotonbori, T 06 6211 0201

Fujiya 1935

Fourth-generation chef Tetsuya Fujiwara trained in Italy and Spain before opening this 19-seat restaurant in 2003. It's a multi-sensory experience: a dark foyer acts as a decompression chamber, with an ambient soundtrack and steel water sculpture that mimics raindrops falling on the leaves of the lotus plant. The minimal second-floor dining area has been fitted out by Osaka studio Mimasis with 'SR-01' walnut chairs from Takayama firm Kitani, designed by Sigurd Resell. The cooking here deserves its two Michelin star rating. Many of the seasonal dishes, such as firefly squid pasta or seared duck breast with wasabi leaves, are made with produce sourced from the Kansai region, including *watarigani* (blue crab) and *ayu* (sweetfish) from Lake Biwa. *2-4-14 Yariyamachi, T 06 6941 2483, www.fujiya1935-osaka.com*

Wad

This charming multistorey teahouse and gallery offers lovely views of the Organic Building (see p076), as well as an insight into Japanese ceramics and *kintsugi*, the noble art of repairing broken pottery. Its selection of brews come largely from the farms in nearby Wazuka and Uji. You can select the receptacle in which your tea is served. Loose-leaf is available to buy.
4-9-3 Minamisemba, T 06 4708 3616

Yoshino Sushi

This culinary institution, in operation since 1841, is the birthplace of Osaka's signature *hakozushi* sushi (Tokyo-style hand-pressed *nigiri* came later). Here, Takuji Hashimoto places rice into a square cypress box, tops it with an assortment of cooked and cured fish and seafood, omelette and soy-braised shiitake mushrooms, and firmly closes the lid to create his multi-coloured geometric savoury morsels. Its well-trodden entrance offers no hint there is a pristine, modern upper floor (above). Tradition is also key at Sushidokoro Amano (T 06 6454 7008), and that's clear even before you eat – its sign is by celebrated Karatsu-ware potter Sajiro Tanaka. The eight seats at Yoshihiro Amano's L-shaped cedar counter are highly coveted for his *nigiri* (the local halfbeak is a special treat) and intricate starters.
3-1-14 Awaji-cho, T 06 6231 7181

Ajikitcho Bunbuan

Though based in a subterranean concourse of Honmachi Station, this peaceful eaterie borrows from the traits of *sukiya-zukuri* (a type of residential architecture), making it quintessentially Japanese and a surprising contrast to all the melee above. Conceived as a *tsuboniwa* (courtyard garden) by local firm Y's Design, interiors bring the outside inside. There are native trees and bamboo fences, and *aji ishi* (diamond granite) walls encircle the darkwood tables; five tatami rooms (above) are more intimate. Keisuke Mifune's three set-course menus feature dishes such as scallops and pickled 'fat cucumber', and grilled *ayu* with rock salt. Order the *omakase* to luxuriate in the full experience. Sister venue Ajikitcho Horie (T 06 6543 1741) opened way back in 1970. *B1F, 3-6-4 Honmachi, T 06 6245 1055, www.ajikitcho.jp*

Moto Coffee

You're never far from water in this city, yet for way too long the canals and rivers that dissect Osaka were covered up or forgotten about. Moto opened in 2010 in a five-storey building and was one of the first river cafés in Kitahama. Many have followed since, but this gem, with its strong brews and a bijou waterside terrace overlooking the Tosabori, has always been popular. The beans come from Coffee Kajita, a venerable roaster in Nagoya. Push the boat out and try a *genmai* (brown-rice coffee), together with a bagel from Ameen's Oven, or perhaps a slice of homemade cheesecake. The bread comes fresh from Boulangerie Mille Village and Mampuku Bakery, and the herbal teas are courtesy of perfumer Rie Ishida. There is another outpost next to Shelf (see p088).
2-1-1 Kitahama, T 06 4706 3788,
www.shelf-keybridge.com

Ñ

Bringing a splash of Mediterranean flair to the Honmachi business district, Hirotomo Sunada worked in kitchens in Madrid and San Sebastián before launching Ñ in 2015. His 15-course menus are updated monthly according to the ingredients of the season. On offer there might be a chilled *salpicón* soup of abalone and local peas; sardines wrapped in aubergine and prepared in a Super Aladín smoker; or Ibérico spare ribs slow-cooked in sherry vinegar and broth, served with a burdock-root confit. There's a strong selection of Spanish wine, as you would expect – we recommend the 2009 Vega Sicilia Único. The 14-cover restaurant has a counter of African teak and 'PP503' chairs by Hans Wegner. Matcha-green walls and exposed brick lend it a homely feel.
Estem Plaza Honmachi Cross,
T 06 6265 1420, www.enye.jp

Mole & Hosoi Coffees

Tatsuya Hosoi's coffee shop is tucked away in the old basement vault of the Shibakawa Building, which was constructed in 1927 as offices for the scion of a trading family but actually served as a girls' finishing school from 1929 to 1943. The former classrooms now host some of Osaka's hippest creators and retail ventures, including eyewear label The Stage (see p092), glassware specialist Ricordo and ceramic artist Yumiko Iihoshi.

Hosoi moved here in 2008. Retro furniture dons Buff Stock Yard did the subtle fit-out, installing a custom-built oak chest, a steel counter and leather stools salvaged from a hotel. The venue has retained a clandestine ambience – you enter through the original reinforced door, and the sandwiches and drip coffee pull in the local scenesters.
*3-3-3 Fushimimachi, T 06 6232 3616,
www.mole-and-hosoicoffees.com*

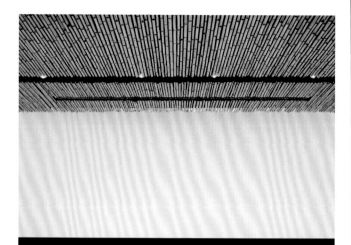

Sagan

Run by the team behind renowned French eaterie Le Pont De Ciel (T 06 6947 0888), this restaurant is found in the basement of Obayashi's former waterfront HQ. Designed by architect Hidehiko Hiramatsu, the 1926 early modernist building shows hallmarks of the Spanish style popular in the US at the time in its decorative terracotta. Tokyo firm Atelier G&B has given Sagan a sultry *jazu kissa* (jazz café) mood, reinforced by low lighting and a baby grand, and installed an African rosewood counter and a textured clay wall that evokes the river outside. The kitchen prides itself in creative dishes made with seasonal ingredients. The well-priced set menu might encompass fried lobster with *daikokushimeji* mushrooms, or rolled cutlassfish with onion and Japanese ginger.
B1, Le Pont De Ciel Building,
6-9 Kitahama-Higashi, T 06 6947 0789

Wasabi

One of Osaka's most well-known dishes, the cheap-and-cheerful *kushikatsu*, is lifted to fine-dining levels at Takako Imaki's Wasabi. She perfected her culinary skills in France and, although the chef says there's nothing Gallic about her cuisine, foie gras and frog don't turn up on *kushikatsu* skewers often. Nor do many chefs of this deep-fried fare tailor sauces to their ingredients. There is no menu here: settle in at one of the nine counter seats and the servings will simply keep on coming (and the bill will continue to escalate) until you state otherwise. Its creative pairings and sleek contemporary interior led to a Michelin star in 2011. Wash your meal down with a draft Suntory beer. Experience the other end of the street-food spectrum in rough-and-ready Shinsekai.
1-1-17 Namba, T 06 6212 6666,
www.hozenji-wasabi.jp

Inc & Sons

With its leather booths and banquettes, exposed concrete walls and bar topped with polished steel, laidback cocktail lounge Inc & Sons, launched by Yasuaki Fuji in 2016, is certainly easy on the eye, but the acoustics here are as important as the chic aesthetics. There's a stash of some 3,000 records, mostly jazz, funk and soul, which are played through a vintage sound system. Libations have included the Golden Club (vanilla-infused aquavit, figs, Cynar, ginger cordial, lemon juice and fennel extract), a favourite in autumn, and a twist on Irish coffee in winter. Pair with seasonal small plates like stout-simmered pork ribs or fried soft-shell crab. Local oysters are on the menu year-round. Open 5pm until 3am.
B1F, CMB Building, 2-3-12 Awajimachi,
T 06 6228 1114, www.inc-sons.com

Mochisho Shizuku

Osaka's most elegant confectionery store specialises in *daifuku* – balls of sticky rice containing bean paste, chestnuts or fruit. Confectioner Yoshihiro Ishida doesn't use artificial additives and makes everything from scratch. He begins work before dawn, pounding rice with a mortar and pestle and then rolling flavours such as black soybean and mochi with Japanese mugwort or hemp charcoal, plus seasonal treats like gingko, strawberry and chocolate. His Kishiwada shop has an old-fashioned decor but this outpost is radically different. The austere interior conceived by Teruhiro Yanagihara (see p054) features an 8m-long concrete table and walls clad in mortar or oxidised black iron. Note that by the afternoon, the most popular varieties have often sold out. *1-17-17 Shinmachi, T 06 6536 0805, www.nichigetsumochi.jp*

Ambrosia and Sakaisuji Club

Designed by the German-trained architect Matakichi Yabe, this Western-style building was completed for the Kawasaki Chochiku Bank back in 1931. These days it provides an elegant and atmospheric setting for Italian trattoria Ambrosia (above), which occupies the ground floor under a soaring ceiling, and French restaurant Sakaisuji Club, set in the more intimate former vaults above (the boardrooms can be booked for private soirées). The set-course dinner menus at the latter kick off at ¥7,000 and offer a series of decadent dishes such as Wagyu steak with foie gras and sauce Périgueux. Another vault has been turned into a wine cellar, which is stocked with French labels including Despagne's Girolate, a sauvignon blanc and semillon blend from Bordeaux. *1-15-12 Minamisemba, T 06 6265 8000, www.sakaisujiclub.com*

Fukutatei

Osaka chef Hiroshi Ukai worked alongside the renowned Gualtiero Marchesi in Milan before launching his Michelin-starred ode to beef. A custom-built clay-brick oven fed by *bincho-tan* (white charcoal) generates temperatures of up to 800°C. Ukai sources his Wagyu solely from female cows, from farms across Japan, more concerned about the quality than production area. For his signature dish, bone-in cutlet, a nod to his mentor, the veal comes from Brittany and is coated in panko breadcrumbs. The other major indulgence here is wine — there are around 200 labels, served in glassware by Lobmeyr and Riedel. Fukutatei is located in Kitanshinshi, an enclave of fine-dining, hostess bars, lounges and private clubs.
B1F, Kitashinchi Star Building, 1-11-19 Sonezaki-Shinchi, T 06 6341 8588, www.fukutatei.com

Noguchi Taro

Kyotoite Taro Noguchi studied in the UK and worked as a salaryman in Tokyo before he opened his restaurant, hidden on the third floor of a nondescript building. It seats 10 diners twice a day. The seasonal 14-course menus – the star of which is the signature wingtips, comprised of free-range chicken broiled over *bincho-tan* – won it a Michelin star within 18 months of its 2009 launch. The cooking is done before your eyes, and dishes like *nodoguro maki,* featuring local blackthroat seaperch grilled on straw, are passed directly from the chef's hands into yours. Unique tableware by ceramicist Jun Kawajiri adorns the walls and helps make for a singular experience. Reservations are required (and tough to come by). However, from 11.30pm until 2am it turns into a bar, serving sake, Japanese whisky and wine.
3F, 1-3-1 Sonezaki-Shinchi, T 06 4796 8222

INSIDER'S GUIDE

TERUHIRO YANAGIHARA, DESIGNER

Born in Kagawa, Teruhiro Yanagihara moved to Osaka to study and stayed, launching his studio in 2002. 'I feel comfortable in a place where history and innovation intertwine,' he says. 'Osaka has been a commercial hub since the Edo period built around its rivers. They divide it into distinct areas, each with its own special character.'

Most mornings, Yanagihara has an organic flat white at Mill Pour (3-6-1 Minamisemba, T 06 6241 1339). He often has lunch at Udon Kyutaro (3-1-16 Kyutaromachi, T 080 2516 2680), which specialises in noodles, followed by dessert at Mochisho Shizuku (see p050), for which he created the interior. 'It's worth queuing for the *momo* (peach) *daifuku*. It also displays art by Hiroshi Sugimoto and Yayoi Kusama.' For retail, he heads to the reborn Daimaru (see p009), a 1933 department store by architect William Merrell Vories: 'Stop by Fiveism x Three, the first men's cosmetic brand in Japan.'

In the evening, he suggests trying a glass of organic wine from a boutique producer at Fujimaru (1-4-18 Higashi-Shinsaibashi, T 06 6258 3515) and the 'finest beef from the grill' at Itamae Yakiniku Itto (1-16-26 Higashi-Shinsaibashi, T 06 6258 2939) before a nightcap at stylish bar Kawana (1-1-8 Namba, T 06 6213 5245), designed by Noi Shigemasa, near Hozenji Yokocho temple (see p024). For further recommendations, he says: 'Ask people sat next to you. Locals are friendly, they'll tell you the best places. In Osaka, many are hidden.' *For full addresses, see Resources.*

ART AND DESIGN

GALLERIES, STUDIOS AND PUBLIC SPACES

The Osaka region was a major hub in the emergence of postwar art in Japan. The hugely influential Gutai movement (see p059) led by painter Jiro Yoshihara was formed in 1954 in neighbouring Ashiya and took a radical approach, pushing beyond the abstract painting of the day. Its members included Kazuo Shiraga, Akira Kanayama, Saburo Murakami and Shozo Shimamoto. The collective's crowning achievement was its participation in the 1970 Osaka world expo (see p068), where it choreographed an art performance featuring men levitating on huge balloons and a bubble-blowing fire truck. View works by the group at Art U (3-2-24 Kitahama, T 06 6201 0221).

Although the city does not have a cohesive art district, creatives have been setting up studios in the south in a vast former shipyard, now known as Creative Center Osaka (4-1-55 Kitakagaya, T 06 4702 7085), since the millennium. Among today's luminaries are Kenji Yanobe, whose anime-esque mechanical sculptures address the theme of survival following a nuclear holocaust, and Yasumasa Morimura, an appropriation artist who inserts himself into iconic images. Art Osaka is a summer highlight, and its setting is both odd and endearing: local powerhouses including Artcourt (see p028), Tezukayama (see p058), Yoshiaki Inoue (see p059) and Nomart (see p060) commandeer the 26th floor of Hotel Granvia (3-1-1 Umeda, T 06 6344 1235) and about 70 rooms are turned into display spaces. *For full addresses, see Resources.*

Kräfte

Inspired by Mies van der Rohe's less-is-more philosophy, Yukio Kimura set up his interior and product design studio Kräfte in 2005, and creates minimal pieces that often have a quirky twist. The 'KK Chair', for example, is all dark clean lines with no visible joints, aside from one decorative white leg. The sleek 'KK0210 Chair' (above) features a deep seat atop an angled frame. Its matte-finished body is made from local larch, and its black iron skeleton has a baked *kobishoku* finish, which gives it an appearance similar to that of brass and will form a patina over time. Kimura has also fitted out a number of Osaka shops, including fashion boutique Freedom From Commonsense (see p086). Email or call to book an appointment to visit the studio.
3-18-1 Nakatsu, T 06 6375 8368,
www.mdnc-krafte.com

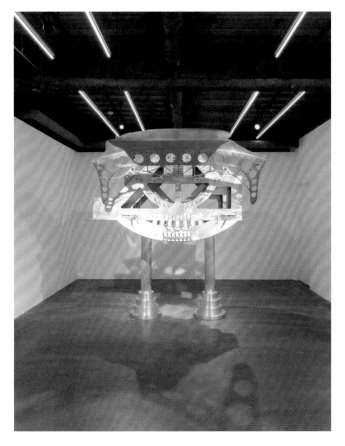

Tezukayama Gallery

Christened after Tezukayama, where it was founded in 1992, Ryoichi Matsuo's boutique gallery moved to its current site in 2010. Its focus has evolved from highlighting global names to championing Japanese up-and-comers, such as mixed-media star Misato Kurimune, known for her rich paintings on monochrome fabric-printed photographs, and local Yoshiyuki Ooe, whose cheerfully macabre sculptures feature skulls, animal parts and strange forms. More established artists are also presented here, including Morio Shinoda: 'Tension and Compression' (above) was his debut commercial outing in Osaka. The main space hosts about seven exhibitions each year. International works, group shows and pieces from the collection are rotated in the Viewing Gallery.

2F, Yamazaki Building, 1-19-27 Minami-Horie, T 06 6534 3993, www.tezukayama-g.com

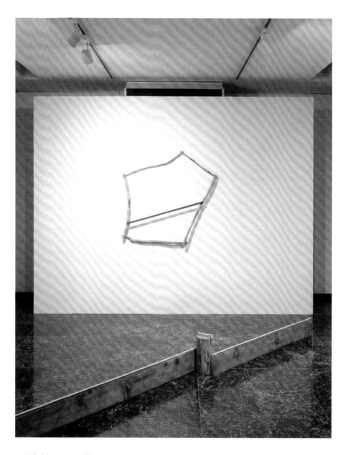

Yoshiaki Inoue Gallery

A welcome breather from the consumerism around it, this gallery has been operating in Shinsaibashi for more than 30 years. Its curator-owner Yoshiaki Inoue works closely with emerging artists to develop long-term relationships. Recent shows have featured Shiga-based Hiroto Kitagawa's anime-like glazed ceramic figurines; photography by Osaka-born Hiroko Inoue; Korean Lee Yun-bok's svelte stainless-steel sculptures; and 'pattern paintings' by Californian Robert Kushner. Exhibitions also present works by established figures such as local treasure Etsuko Nakatsuji, who plays with the human form, as well as Jiro Yoshihara, Sadamasa Motonaga and Takesada Matsutani of the Gutai group. Inoue is one of the movers and shakers of the annual Art Osaka fair.
2F, 1-3-10 Shinsaibashi-suji,
T 06 6245 5347, www.gallery-inoue.com

Nomart Gallery

Founded as a publishing studio by director Satoshi Hayashi in 1989, Nomart – a canny portmanteau of 'nomad' and 'art' reflecting its independent ethos – is now a full-scale creative enterprise comprising a silkscreen-printing studio, a graphic design house and a gallery. It is located in a small shed with a sloping roof that has been squeezed in between brick apartment blocks. For the 30th anniversary exhibition (opposite), it showed pieces by 30 artists, among them Kobe-born sculptor Keiji Uematsu, Kyoto printer and photo-engraver Hideki Kimura and Okayama installation specialist Kodai Nakahara, alongside local Kohei Nawa. He is known for his 'PixCell' series, in which he affixes glass spheres to items like taxidermy deer, lending them an ethereal shimmer.

3-5-22 Nagata, Joto-ku, T 06 6964 2323, www.nomart.co.jp

The Third Gallery Aya

Founded by Tomoko Aya in 1996 as a space for photography, The Third Gallery's scope has widened to comprise video, drawing and painting but its original focus remains. As an incubator for Kansai's emerging and mid-career female artists, it has featured notable names such as Hiromi Kakimoto, whose portraits blur fantasy and reality, and Midori Komatsubara, who is known for her well-observed stills based on the *yaoi* media genre. 'Flash Memories' (above) presented Osakan street snapper Jun Abe's monochromatic images (left) and Ishiuchi Miyako's 'Hiroshima' series (right) depicting clothing and other artefacts that survived the bombing in 1945. Under Aya's direction, works have been added to major museum collections, including MOMAT in Tokyo.
2F, Wakasa Building, 1-8-24 Edobori, T 06 6445 3557, www.thethirdgalleryaya.com

Truck

It's a bit of a trek to Truck and there's little else to see nearby, but it's worth the effort to reach what is Osaka's most interesting furniture shop. Husband-and-wife team Tokuhiko Kise and Hiromi Karatsu design the pieces together, then Kise figures out how to build them. The duo's creations are characterful but unfussy, and utilise oak, brass and iron. They have a penchant for what they call 'furrowed leather', made from Japanese hides soaked in tannins to bring out the texture, then softened with fish oils. The products aren't sold in other stores, but they can be made to order and shipped. After a look around, head across the street to Bird Coffee (T 06 6958 1616), their hip café that showcases Truck pieces. Closed Tuesdays and some Wednesdays.
*6-8-48 Shinmori, T 06 6958 7055,
www.truck-furniture.co.jp*

ARCHITOUR

A GUIDE TO OSAKA'S ICONIC BUILDINGS

A relaxed attitude to urban planning has not always served Osaka well, but this hands-off approach has given enlightened CEOs and municipal officials the freedom to commission some exceptional concepts. Cesar Pelli has designed three city landmarks, including The National Museum of Art (see p029), one of his most recognised works, and the high-rise Abeno Harukas (see p012). Friedensreich Hundertwasser turned an incinerator into something resembling a fairground ride (see p074), while Tadao Ando's many creations scattered across the region include Galleria Akka (1-16-20 Higashi-Shinsaibashi) and the Prefectural Chikatsu-Asuka Museum (see p103). Add to this a growing collection of structures by the current Japanese vanguard – Hiroshi Hara (see p011), Kengo Kuma (see p077) and Jun Aoki, who inserted a serene wedding chapel into the grounds of the Hyatt Regency (1-13-11 Nanko-Kita, Suminoe-ku).

Investment seems to swing from north to south every couple of decades, and at present the north is rising. The Umeda district around Osaka Station hadn't had a facelift since the bubble era, but railway and construction giants have spent the past 15 years packing the area with multipurpose complexes, and development is ongoing. To view pre-WWII architecture, check out Norin Kaikan (see p095) and head over to Kitahama (see p069), where numerous 1920s and 1930s buildings were funded by wealthy merchants. *For full addresses, see Resources.*

Namba Parks

Until the 1990s, Namba was the rundown site of an old baseball stadium – the only reason to visit was Doguya-suji, a shopping strip where chefs still go to buy knives and other utensils. Today, the area is a genuine hub and something of an oasis in the dense centre. Over a 3.4-hectare tract of land next to Namba train station, Los Angeles-based architects Jerde (who were part-responsible for the successful Roppongi Hills project in Tokyo) created an expanse of trees, lawns and ponds that are set around a 30-storey tower and a handful of smaller buildings housing more than 120 retail outlets. It was completed in 2003. To fully appreciate the architecture on show, ascend to the Parks Garden urban farm on the ninth floor, from where you will have a bird's-eye view.
2-10-70 Nambanaka, T 06 6644 7100, www.nambaparks.com

Osaka Culturarium at Tempozan

Built in 1994 on the harbour, this Tadao Ando cultural complex (formerly known as the Suntory Museum) perfectly shows off the local architect's consummate use of concrete, mastery of natural light and sensitivity towards nature. It is made up of three overlapping geometric volumes. The biggest, a truncated upturned cone of glass and steel, engulfs a podium that houses an Imax cinema and shop. From here, two rectangular structures project out along different axes towards the bay, each fronted by a wall of windows that frame dramatic views. In the larger one, an art museum hosts extensive displays of Japanese posters and comics. A plaza featuring a semi-circular amphitheatre connects the complex to the water below. *1-5-10 Kaigan-dori, Minato-ku, T 06 6586 3911, www.osaka-c-t.jp*

Tower of the Sun

Taro Okamoto's surreal 70m-tall sculpture faces the Expo '70 Commemorative Park gates, through which more than 64 million visitors passed that year. A former student at the Sorbonne in Paris, where he mixed with the likes of Georges Bataille and Max Ernst, Okamoto occupied an unusual role in Japan – a serious writer and artist who also appeared as a comic on knockabout TV shows until his death in 1996. *Tower of the Sun* is his most famous work and one of hardly any original Expo structures to still be standing. Another is *The Moon World* by Isamu Noguchi, a cratered sphere that few would guess was by the Japanese-American artist. Also check out the National Museum of Ethnology (see p070) and stroll the 10m-high wood walkway through the treetops.
1-1 Senri Banpaku Koen, Suita-shi,
T 06 6877 7387, www.expo70-park.jp

Ikoma Building

This stately art deco pile is an example of early modern architecture in the Kitahama district. Completed in 1930, the reinforced concrete structure cost ¥150,000 – one of the most expensive in the city at the time. Its architect Heizo So (also responsible for the 1912 Naniwa Bridge) was inspired by the soon-to-be tenants, watchmaker G Ikoma: the bay windows on the tower's third to fifth floors and a circular window on the second resemble the pendulum of a grandfather clock. Seven granite eagle sculptures stand sentry on the facade. The interior has been updated but some original features remain, including the Italian marble staircase and stained glass windows. There is now a café at ground level and offices above. Weekday tours take place between 9am and 5pm.
2-2-12 Hirano-cho, T 06 6231 0751, www.ikoma.ne.jp

National Museum of Ethnology
This huge museum, known colloquially as
Minpaku, communicates Kisho Kurokawa's
belief that buildings should 'evolve' thanks
to alterations and additions. Constructed
in the Expo '70 Commemorative Park and
opened in 1977, it shows more than 12,000
pieces that are drawn from a pool of about
350,000 global artefacts. Its mission is to
champion cultural diversity, and 11 galleries
spotlight everyday items and local customs
from the Americas to Oceania. The Japan
section details the development of fishery,
hunting and agriculture on the archipelago.
The design concept of a series of 'capsules'
(structures set in a courtyard that allow for
flexibility) is one Kurokawa often explored.
The turrets (above) and bulging, rounded
corners are also typical of his style, and
presage the shift to more fluid forms that
occurred as postmodernism developed.
10-1 Senri Banpaku Koen, Suita-shi,
T 06 6876 2151, www.minpaku.ac.jp

The Symphony Hall

Devised by Taisei Corporation and built in 1982 to mark the 30th anniversary of the Asahi Broadcasting Corporation (see p077), this was the first concert hall in the country to be designed solely for playing Western-style classical music (no moveable stages or orchestra pits here). Each aspect of the interiors, from the cork floor to the sound-reflecting ceiling boards, was selected to enhance the sophisticated acoustics that it is celebrated for. At full capacity, it has a reverberation time of two seconds, which is considered optimal for Bach, Mozart et al. The 1,704 seats are strategically arranged on all sides, edging the stage and helping to create an experience that is also visually exciting. To the rear is a magnificent organ crafted by Kuhn of Switzerland, with three keyboards, 54 stops and 3,732 pipes.
2-3-3 Oyodominami, T 06 6453 1010

Osaka City Museum of Fine Arts

Located in Tennoji Park, this tranquil site was donated to the city by the Sumitomo family of merchants in 1926. Established a decade later, the museum's mission is to enrich the lives of Osakans through culture. Spread across a three-storey building and two underground levels, it hosts temporary exhibitions and permanent collections. The latter incorporates more than 8,400 pieces of Japanese and Chinese painting, craft and sculpture, much of which has been granted national-treasure status. At the back of the building is the noted Keitakuen Garden by Jihei Ogawa (aka Ueji, one of the country's finest landscapers). At its centre is a large pond with its own island. Allow the bridges, paths, stepping stones and artificial hills to guide you through it. Closed Mondays.

1-8-2 Chausuyama-cho, T 06 6771 4874,
www.osaka-art-museum.jp

Maishima Incineration Plant

Few waste plants attract tourists, but then few have been created by the late Viennese artist and environmentalist Friedensreich Hundertwasser. This ecologically minded state-of-the-art garbage disposal facility opened in 2001, and its novel look came as a result of the city sprucing up its image in a bid to host the 2008 Olympics. It's made over with colourful free-flowing forms (the Austrian famously rejected straight lines), and has 500 windows – about 100 of which are real – and a 120m-tall chimney topped with an attention-grabbing golden orb. The aesthetic is part postmodern, part thrilling theme park, which explains why it's often mistaken for the nearby Universal Studios. Apply for a free tour to see Hundertwasser's artworks inside, and to get up on the roof. *1-2-48 Hokkoshiratsu, T 06 6463 4153, www.osaka-env-paa.jp*

Organic Building

Gaetano Pesce made a substantial impact internationally in 1969 with his 'Up' line of furniture, and has created pieces for Vitra and B&B Italia. The New York-based Italian has also designed a sprinkling of enigmatic edifices, the most admired of which is this nine-storey office block completed in 1993. Constructed for *konbu* seaweed wholesaler Oguraya Yamamoto, the building is clad in 132 organically shaped fibreglass funnels planted with 80 types of indigenous flora, all watered via a computerised hydration system. The structure was declared a civic landmark a year after its completion, and city leaders agreed to the responsibility of managing the vertical garden. Today, it is a popular reference point. For the best views skip across the junction to Wad (see p038), a specialist tea café and gallery space.

4-7-21 Minamisemba

Asahi Broadcasting Corporation

Osaka-based ABC offered Kengo Kuma a prime 8,500 sq m footprint to utilise for its new headquarters. His waterfront design is dramatic, accessible and sustainable. The chequered facade made from reconstituted timber evokes an old Japanese puzzle box but serves a practical purpose too: it allows the river breeze to cool the building in the winter and to limit heat absorption in the warmer months. Rather than a secure fort, Kuma wanted to create architecture that Osakans could connect with. He conceived a grand open-air staircase to guide visitors through the heart of the structure and on to a riverside deck. The ABC Hall, operated by Asahi, hosts a variety of arts events and live performances. Head to Nakanoshima on the opposite side of the Dojima for the clearest views of the 2008 complex.
1-1-30 Fukushima

Boat Park Suminoe

Established in 1952, *kyotei* (boat racing) is a beloved spectator sport, and not just for the speed; betting on the outcome is one of Japan's few legal forms of gambling. From a flying start, six colour-coded hydroplanes hare three times around a 600m elliptical course, which takes 120 seconds or so. The vessels are randomly allocated to drivers on the day, about 10 per cent of whom are women and regularly participate in mixed-gender events (but rarely win; the national culture dictates that they don't embarrass the men). Opened in 1956, the freshwater stadium at Suminoe holds 21,000 and has free and paid-for seats, depending on the comfort. Stats and results are colourfully displayed on a gigantic scoreboard. Races run from early afternoon until about 9pm. *1-1-71 Izumi, Suminoe-ku, T 06 6685 5112, www.boatrace-suminoe.jp*

SHOPS

THE BEST RETAIL THERAPY AND WHAT TO BUY

Centuries before Japan began commercial relations with the West in the 19th century, the Sakai area of Osaka prefecture was peddling swords and copper to China and South-East Asia. And although it's just old men who still greet each other with *Mokarimakka?* ('Have you turned a profit?'), locals continue to bring products to market. This was the first city to sell calculators, TVs and camera phones.

Over the past 15 years, developers have been pouring money into multipurpose complexes such as Herbis Plaza (2-5-25 Umeda, T 06 6343 7500), Abeno Harukas (see p012) and Namba Parks (see p065). The most notable has been the vast Grand Front (T 06 6372 6300), inaugurated in 2013, with a Knowledge Capital area in which companies and researchers show off visions of the future.

Other retail zones have grown more organicially as independents cluster together. Minamisemba offers the most refined choice, with a flagship Issey Miyake (see p084) and honeypots such as Norin Kaikan (see p095), a 1930 corporate HQ packed with fashion and arts outlets. Horie, encompassing the lifestyle boutiques on Orange Street (see p083), is dotted with chic one-offs. And Nakazakicho is an eclectic mix of century-old *nagaya* populated by craft stores and cafés interspersed with contemporary spaces like Mook (opposite). The only obstacle is the baffling address system, in which smaller streets go unnamed and numbering needs a maths PhD to decipher. *For full addresses, see Resources.*

Mook

Amid the streets of Nakazakicho, a district dotted with an unusual number of *nagaya* (traditional terraced houses) as a result of it being missed in the 1945 bombings, this stylish salon is a bastion of calm in a busy city. Renovated by local architect Takeshi Okuwada in 2015, its chamfered entrance and polished concrete floors lead into an enclosed space clad in untreated oak. The irregular panels, which are positioned so that their grain runs in the same direction as the light streaming in through the glass frontage, also have a secondary benefit: they absorb some of the natural humidity that comes with running the shop. A cut and colour will set you back ¥9,900, after which, head out, slump into a comfortable armchair and enjoy lunch at nearby café Taiyonotou Green West (T 06 6131 4400).
4-3-40 Nakazakinishi, www.mook-hair.com

Fukuju Blue Label

From its headquarters in Kobe, Fukuju has been producing sake from rice sown in the north of Hyogo since 1751. Its *junmai ginjo* Blue Label is fermented at low temperature for long periods and is aromatic with a silky melon and apricot palate. The ultramarine bottle and branding by local studio Ai-Kobo makes it a great gift. However, for yourself, seek out Akishika, the jewel of the Kansai scene, founded in Osaka in 1886. Its sixth-generation head brewer Hiroaki Oku uses organic rice (if it has been grown by him personally, bottles are stamped with a red face), does not filter and makes only the *junmai* (pure) category, with nothing else but yeast, water and *koji*. The conventional wisdom is that sake should be drunk fresh and finished soon after opening. Akishika has a structure that improves for years. *www.enjoyfukuju.com*

Biotop

Like many Minami-Horie haunts, Biotop is both a lifestyle store and a café. Work your way up from the ground floor, which carries botanicals and local homeware brands like Starnet and Hippopotamus, and hosts the hole-in-the-wall coffee stop Corner Stand, whose beans come from specialists Pretty Things. You will notice plenty of exposed concrete and steel while moving through the industrial interiors, installed by Tokyo studio Suppose Design Office, especially on the second floor (above), with its mirrored display units. Here there is womenswear and menswear from Osaka labels Auralee, Takahiromiyashita the Soloist and Fumika Uchida. On the fourth level is a lush roof terrace replete with potted plants, where Cubierta serves excellent wood-fired pizza.
1/2/4F, 1-16-1 Minami-Horie,
T 06 6531 8223, www.biotop.jp/osaka

Issey Miyake
The world's biggest Issey Miyake store opened in 2019 and houses all eight of the designer's sub-brands. The modern minimalist aesthetic courtesy of Shingo Noma riffs on the city's relationship with water. There are stainless-steel railings that resemble U-bends, sofas that look like bars of soap and, outside, a massive gleaming tap head above the entrance.
4-11-28 Minamisemba, T 06 6251 8887

Freedom From Commonsense

Toshiyuki Aoyama opened his multi-brand boutique in 2013. It's mostly menswear on the racks, but the overriding style is casual and loose-fitting and many of the garments have a unisex appeal. The predominantly Japanese items include sandals and desert boots from Ptarmigan, embroidered cotton tees from Ryo Matsuoka, baggy wool knits by Yashiki, and bags courtesy of Kiruna, as well as beauty products by Cul de Sac, and a covetable range of accessories such as Shosa wallets and business-card holders by No, No, Yes!. Kräfte (see p057) devised the blindingly white space, meant to immerse shoppers in Aoyama's world. To find it, look for fashion store People Have The Power (T 06 6281 8456) at the front of the block. *2F, Taguchi Building, 4-6-3 Minamisemba, T 06 6241 4570, www.freedom-from-commonsense.com*

Howse/Buddy Optical

Eyewear designer Gen Ikehara's impeccable taste is on full display in this dual-purpose concept store. Buddy Optical is the name of his modish line of specs, manufactured in Fukui prefecture and presented on bespoke plywood units by local architect Yasunari Tsukada. Two of the most popular models are the 'Sorbonne', which nods to preppy style with its flattened round frames, and the semi-rimless 'TUB', made of titanium and acetate, that draws inspiration from midcentury Germany. Howse touts items by brands that have caught Ikehara's fancy, such as bags by Fukuoka enterprise Kaili and butterfly-hunting jackets by Aichi label Tehu Tehu. Collaborations with Tokyo-based curators Kian have given rise to pop-ups by the likes of ceramicist Anna Beam.
2F, 1-13-24 Kyomachibori, T 06 6147 8834, www.howsebuddyoptical.com

Shelf

Launched by the team responsible for the neighbouring Moto Coffee (see p042), this repository for contemporary crafts stocks pieces created by artisans from around the country, many of which are put to good use at Moto. You might come across stripped-back wooden utensils by Niigatan Takashi Tomii, ceramics by Tetsuya Otani, made in his studio in historic pottery hub Shigaraki, woven bamboo baskets by Ojiro Kakumono

Ten or vases hand-blown by Osakan Takara Kinoshita, displayed on unobtrusive shelves and counters. Previous rotating exhibitions have highlighted Kayo Miyashita's wire-and-paper mobiles and stylish cloth bags from Momota Mutsumi. One non-native maker featured is Peter Ivy, based in Toyama and known for his quirkily imperfect glassware.
2-1-2 Uchihonmachi, T 06 6355 4783, www.shelf-keybridge.com

Graf

In 2000, a product designer, a carpenter, a furniture-maker, a chef, an architect and an artist formed interdisciplinary collective Decorative Mode No 3, retailing under the brand name Graf. The group creates unique, understated items, from furniture, such as the exquisitely crafted nara-wood 'Round Stool', to kitchen accessories: the whimsical 'Cut Piece' series features brass chopstick rests modelled (and stacked) like slices of onion and a bottle opener in the shape of a lotus root. There are collaborations too. The KG-amp (above, ¥207,000), produced together with Komatsu Acoustic Research Laboratory and encased in ivory and teak, looks as good as it sounds. The showroom encompasses a café serving veggie dishes made with produce sourced all over Japan.
4-1-1 Nakanoshima, T 06 6459 2100, www.graf-d3.com

Especial Records

Brothers Yoshihiro and Shuya Okino, who make up the renowned Kyoto Jazz Massive, are based in Osaka and Tokyo respectively. While Shuya added radio DJ and writer to his resumé, Yoshihiro started this record shop and label. As you might expect, this is no ordinary music store. Especial Records feels like a friend's house that just happens to stock some of the best and rarest house, hip hop and nu jazz tracks in Japan. The store is tiny but scour the racks and you'll find a well-curated collection of new and secondhand CDs and vinyl – look out for Sleep Walker, Ronin Arkestra, Nayutah and Mitsu The Beats. When Yoshihiro's in town, he might be behind the counter and DJing at various venues; he regularly performs at Metro (T 07 5752 4765) over in Kyoto.
Sakura Building, 4-9-2 Minamisemba,
T 06 6241 0336, www.especial-records.com

The Stage
The city of Sabae produces 95 per cent
of Japan's eyewear, and many of its best
craftsmen work for Kaneko Optical. This
emporium in the Shibakawa Building is
a tribute to their skills and production
techniques. All the frames are handmade
and stamped with the name of the maker.
Over the corridor is a mini-museum that
is dedicated to the history of optometry.
3-3-3 Fushimimachi, T 06 6204 5280

Calo Bookshop and Cafe

This is the ideal place to discover what is happening in Osaka's creative community. Launched by Akiko Ishikawa in 2004, Calo specialises in visual culture and poetry, including 'zines printed in all corners of the country, and further afield in Jakarta and Seoul; you may unearth a photojournal by Atsuko Suzuki, or *KOA*, which spotlights emerging artists from Kyushu and Okinawa. Devised by Teruhiro Yanagihara (see p054), the space is pared down yet inviting, with a raw concrete ceiling and shelving made of lauan veneer. In its gallery, exhibitions showcase regional talent, such as graphic designer Fumio Tachibana and illustrator Kazumi Ozaki. The café serves up Japanese roasted tea and an eclectic mix of foreign fare, like chicken curry with brown rice.

5F, Wakasa Building, 1-8-24 Edobori,
T 06 6447 4777, www.calobookshop.com

Norin Kaikan

Once a low-cost option for cash-strapped retailers, the city's older buildings are now prime real estate. Today, many boutiques want to occupy a 20th-century property, and this 1930 structure probably tops the list. Built for the Mitsubishi Corporation, it was sold to a former agriculture ministry bureaucrat, who renamed it Norin Kaikan (Agriculture and Forestry Hall) and invited in creative companies looking for pastures new. Explore its corridors and you'll find Maison Martin Margiela (T 06 6282 0009) and clothes shop Strato (T 06 6244 1591), as well as Flannagan (T 06 6120 2416), a bookshop that specialises in design titles and stationery, music store Stringphonic (T 06 6120 1828), which sells instruments and records, and other outlets peddling jewellery, craft goods, art and more.
2-6-3 Minamisemba, www.osaka-norin.com

ESCAPES

WHERE TO GO IF YOU WANT TO LEAVE TOWN

Add up the land mass of the 6,852 islands that form the Japanese archipelago and the area is smaller than California. In a nation of 127 million people, this means urban centres are densely packed, but also neighbouring cities are easier to visit than you may think.

Board a *shinkansen* north and you can be in Kyoto in less than 15 minutes. Head an hour outside of the ancient city to discover IM Pei's Miho Museum (300 Tashiro Momodani, T 07 4882 3411), mostly buried in a forested mountainous site in Shiga prefecture. Under an hour east of Osaka is Nara, where sika deer still roam the streets, and the colossal Daibutsu-den, part of the Todaiji temple complex, has stood for 1,200 years. Go west to stay the night at Yodoko Guest House (see p100), reached on the cute Hanshin train from Umeda Station that carries on to Kobe, the capital for five months in 1180. Rejuvenate at nearby Negiya Ryofukaku onsen (see p102) before journeying to the islands of the Seto Inland Sea, which are strewn with art installations. Catch the ferry from Okayama to Naoshima (opposite), from where you can carry on to Inujima (see p098).

Not far south, the Chikatsu Asuka Museum (see p103) is a real hidden gem. A little further but easier to access is Fudouguchikan (7 Ogi, Izumisano-shi, T 07 2459 7326), a traditional hot spring inn nestled beautifully among the tranquillity and greenery of Mount Inunki. Just 60 minutes from the city, it feels like a world away. *For full addresses, see Resources.*

Chichu Art Museum, Kagawa

Tadao Ando's island museum is tucked into the verdant rolling terrain and barely rises above the ground so as not to disturb the site's natural beauty. It's a select, powerful collection, comprising nine works by artists James Turrell, Walter De Maria and Claude Monet (one room is devoted to his 'Water Lilies' series). The concrete corridors and 'courts' linking the galleries cleave through the hillside; some are open to the elements,

and as the visitor moves from inside to out, the sky and the weather become integral to the experience. It's rather evocative of Ken Adam's Bond film-set designs. Closed on Mondays. A sister museum (T 08 7968 3555) on nearby Teshima island displays 'Matrix', an ethereal installation piece by Rei Naito and architect Ryue Nishizawa. *3449-1 Naoshima, T 08 7892 3755, www.benesse-artsite.jp*

Inujima Seirensho Art Museum
The copper refinery on Inujima island was
in operation for just 10 years after opening
in 1909, as the metal's price plummeted.
It was abandoned for nearly nine decades,
until the philanthropist Soichiro Fukutake
repurposed it into an art museum with an
eco slant. To prune environmental impact,
Hiroshi Sambuichi preserved much of the
building and utilised karami bricks made
from slag to construct the four-hall space,
integrating geothermal and solar energy:
you enter via the Earth Gallery, a tunnel
of mirrors illuminated by a skylight. Inside,
artist Yukinori Yanagi's works pay homage
to author Yukio Mishima, who condemned
Japan's rapid industrialisation; fragments
of Mishima's house are suspended in *Solar
Rock* (opposite), part of 'Hero Dry Cell'. Also
check out the Art House Project galleries by
Yuko Hasegawa and Kazuyo Sejima nearby.
*327-4 Inujima, Higashi-ku, T 08 6947 1112,
benesse-artsite.jp/en/art/seirensho.html*

Yodoko Guest House, Ashiya
Frank Lloyd Wright spent seven years in Japan and this 1924 residential building is a crucial part of his legacy. Perched on a hillside, its four storeys of volcanic Oya-ishi stone are framed by greenery. Dozens of small shuttered windows set high up help control light and ventilation. Open on Wednesdays and at weekends.
3-10 Yamate-cho, Hyogo, T 07 9738 1720, www.yodoko-geihinkan.jp

Negiya Ryofukaku

The Arima Onsen resort, an hour by train from Osaka, dates back to the 8th century (it is said that the feudal ruler Toyotomi Hideyoshi liked to recuperate here). The 33-room Negiya Ryofukaku ryokan opened in 1857, and its name references its original purpose – a rest house for Shinto priests. One reason it has lasted so long is that it has modernised without sacrificing any of its character. In a 2010 renovation, design studio Process5 devised four extra rooms, using maple to echo the trees surrounding the inn. They split each of them (Japanese Modern, above) in two, with a tatami-mat area by the entrance and a Western-style sleeping area. Order a traditional tea or dinner, then flop back on the sofa facing the window and the wonderful scenery.
1537-2 Arima-cho, Kita-ku, Hyogo,
T 07 8904 0675, www.negiyaryokan.com

Prefectural Chikatsu Asuka Museum

About a 45-minute drive from Osaka, this fascinating museum shows artefacts from the Kofun and Asuka periods (from the 4th to the 8th century). It's set in the 'valley of mausoleums', which comprises more than 200 burial mounds – including the tumuli of four emperors, as well as state officials and noble families. The striking concrete edifice was designed by Tadao Ando to sit harmoniously within the topography of the natural landscape, designated a historical park. Its elongated sloping stone-paved roof is a monumental stairway that serves as a stage or platform from which to survey the surrounding tombs. Inside, excavated pieces are exhibited in a dimly lit foyer that evokes the crypts in which they were found.
299 Higashiyama, Kanan-cho, Minamikawachi, T 07 2193 8321, www.chikatsu-asuka.jp

NOTES
SKETCHES AND MEMOS

RESOURCES
CITY GUIDE DIRECTORY

HOTELS
ADDRESSES AND ROOM RATES

The Blend Inn 023
Room rates:
double, from ¥8,000
1-24-16 Baika
Konohana-ku
T 070 1745 1250
www.theblend.jp

Conrad 016
Room rates:
double, from ¥51,000
3-2-4 Nakanoshima
T 06 6222 0111
www.conradhotels3.hilton.com

First Cabin 016
Room rates:
double, from ¥9,000
4-2-1 Namba
T 06 6631 8090
www.first-cabin.jp

The Flag 020
Room rates:
double, from ¥12,000;
Deluxe Double, from ¥20,000
1-18-30 Higashi-Shinsaibashi
T 06 6121 8111
www.hoteltheflag.jp

Fudouguchikan 096
Room rates:
prices on request
7 Ogi
Izumisano-shi
T 07 2459 7326
www.fudouguchikan.com

The Grandee 016
Room rates:
prices on request
1-6-28 Higashi-Shinsaibashi
T 06 6251 7170
www.thegrandee.co.jp

Hotel Granvia 056
Room rates:
double, from ¥17,000
3-1-1 Umeda
T 06 6344 1235
www.granvia-osaka.jp

Hyatt Regency 064
Room rates:
double, from ¥17,000
1-13-11 Nanko-Kita
Suminoe-ku
www.hyatt.com

Imperial Hotel 016
Room rates:
double, from ¥18,500
1-8-50 Tenmabashi
T 06 6881 1111
www.imperialhotel.co.jp

Marriott Miyako Hotel 013
Room rates:
double, from ¥26,000
1-1-43 Abeno-suji
T 06 6628 6111
www.marriott.com

Moxy 017
Room rates:
double, from ¥14,500;
Signature Queen, from ¥17,000
2-2-9 Kawaramachi
T 06 6204 5200
www.marriott.com

Negiya Ryofukaku 102
Room rates:
prices on request
1537-2 Arima-cho
Kita-ku
Hyogo
T 07 8904 0675
www.negiyaryokan.com

The New Otani 016
Room rates:
double, from ¥14,000
1-4-1 Shiromi
T 06 6941 1111
www.newotani.co.jp/osaka

Residential Hotel Hare Kuromon 018
Room rates:
prices on request
2-14-32 Nipponbashi
T 06 4394 8708
www.hotelhare.jp/kuromon

The Ritz-Carlton 022
Room rates:
double, from ¥42,000;
Japanese Suite, from ¥91,000
2-5-25 Umeda
T 06 6343 7000
www.ritzcarlton.com/osaka

St Regis 016
Room rates:
double, from ¥30,000
3-6-12 Honmachi
T 06 6258 3333
www.stregisosaka.co.jp

Hotel She 019
Room rates:
double, from ¥11,000
1-2-5 Ichioka
Minato-ku
T 06 6577 5500
www.hotelsheosaka.com

The Westin 016
Room rates:
double, from ¥23,000
1-1-20 Oyodonaka
T 06 6440 1111
www.westin-osaka.co.jp

Yamatoya Honten 016
Room rates:
double, from ¥21,000
2-17-4 Shimanouchi
T 06 6211 3587
www.yamatoyahonten.co.jp

WALLPAPER* CITY GUIDES

Executive Editor
Jeremy Case

Authors
JJ O'Donoghue
Celia Polkinghorne

Photography Editor
Rebecca Moldenhauer

Art Editor
Jade R Arroyo

Senior Sub-Editor
Sean McGeady

Editorial Assistant
Josh Lee

Contributors
Nicholas Coldicott
Federica Sala
Rachael Ward
Japan Institute of Culture
& International Exchange

Interns
Alison Evans
Rashida Jasdanwalla
Anqi La
Alex Merola

Osaka Imprint
First published 2009
Third edition 2020

ISBN 978 1 83866 044 4

More City Guides
www.phaidon.com/travel

Follow us
@wallpaperguides

Contact
wcg@phaidon.com

Original Design
Loran Stosskopf

Map Illustrator
Russell Bell

Production Controller
Gif Jittiwutikarn

**Assistant Production
Controller**
Lily Rodgers

Wallpaper* Magazine
161 Marsh Wall
London E14 9AP
contact@wallpaper.com

Wallpaper*® is a
registered trademark
of TI Media

Phaidon Press Limited
Regent's Wharf
All Saints Street
London N1 9PA

Phaidon Press Inc
65 Bleecker Street
New York, NY 10012

All prices and venue
information are correct
at time of going to press,
but are subject to change.

A CIP Catalogue record for
this book is available from
the British Library.

PHOTOGRAPHERS

Daisuke Shima
Cosmo Tower, p010
Osaka Castle, p015
Moxy Hotel, p017
Residential Hotel Hare
Kuromon, p018
Hotel She, p019
The Flag, p020, p021
The Blend Inn, p023
Ad Hoc, p033
Shuhari, p034
Sumibi Kappo Ishii, p035
Honkogetsu, p036
Fujiya 1935, p037
Wad, pp038-039
Ajikitcho Bunbuan, p041
Moto Coffee, p042, p043
Ñ, p044
Inc & Sons, pp048-049
Fukutatei, p052
Noguchi Taro, p053
Teruhiro Yanagihara, p055
Yoshiaki Inoue Gallery,
p059
Nomart Gallery,
p060, p061
Osaka Culturarium at
Tempozan, pp066-067
Ikoma Building, p069
Osaka City Museum of Fine
Arts, p073
Maishima Incineration
Plant, pp074-075

Boat Park Suminoe,
pp078-079
Biotop, p083
Issey Miyake, pp084-085
Freedom From
Commonsense, p086
Howse/Buddy Optical, p087
Shelf, p088, p089

Yoshiro Masuda
Abeno Harukas, pp012-013
Granknot Coffee
Roasters, p025
Kaara, p031
Yoshino Sushi, p040
Mole & Hosoi Coffees, p045
Wasabi, p047
Mochisho Shizuku, p050
Truck, p063
Namba Parks, p065
The Stage, pp092-093
Norin Kaikan, p095

Christoffer Rudquist
Umeda Sky Building, p011
Glico Man Sign, p014
The Ritz-Carlton, p022
The National Museum
of Art, p029
HEP Five, p030
Sagan, p046
Ambrosia, p051

National Museum of
Ethnology, p070, p071
Organic Building, p076
Especial Records, p091
Calo Bookshop and Cafe,
p094

Daici Ano
Inujima Seirensho Art
Museum, p098, p099

Takeru Koroda
Artcourt Gallery, p028

Mitsuo Matsuoka
Shiba Ryotaro Memorial
Museum, p027
Prefectural Chikatsu Asuka
Museum, p103

Hyogo Mugyuda
Tezukayama Gallery, p058

Seiichi Ohsawa
Chichu Art Museum, p097

Daisuke Shimokawa
Negiya Ryofukaku, p102

Superstock
Shiba Ryotaro Memorial
Museum, p026

OSAKA

A COLOUR-CODED GUIDE TO THE HOT 'HOODS

MINAMI
Neon-tastic streets and hip hangouts mean Minami is as colourful as it is atmospheric

KITA
Skyscrapers vie to outdo each other in this lively district that throngs with teen tribes

NAKANOSHIMA
Osaka's main financial centre is crisscrossed by two rivers, the Tosabori and the Dojima

OSAKA CASTLE
Ancient meets modern where the city's concrete castle overlooks the business park

THE BAY
The old port is being reinvented as a cultural hub replete with dramatic architecture

TENNOJI
Shitennoji Temple is a major draw, as is Abeno Harukas, one of Japan's tallest buildings

For a full description of each neighbourhood, see the Introduction.
Featured venues are colour-coded, according to the district in which they are located.